Disclaimer

The information provided in this file should not be used to treat or consult with any medical condition. For this you should go to a professional doctor. The information provided is an in-depth guide that applies to everyone however individuals should consult a physician to determine which body type they have and which training is best for them. The author accepts no responsibility or liability for the damage or injury of any person alleged to be caused by this programme or any information given by the author.

Contents page

#1: ADAPTATION IS KEY!　　　　　Page 3

#2 "The Best Exercises"　　　　　Page 6

#3 Positions of Flexion　　　　　Page 11

#4 How do I make my workouts more effective?　Page 13

#5 Where should I train?　　　　　Page 15

#6 The actual workouts!　　　　　Page 17

#1: ADAPTATION IS KEY!

The real secret to bodybuilding behind the hours of hard work in the gym is adaptation! Too many bodybuilders sweat it out in the gym day after day doing the same mundane routines simply because they're told "these are the best exercises for this type of training"…utter crap! Yes, there are exercises that are better than others, but at no point should you create a routing and stick to it forever.

The best stimulation and muscle gain is created when the body has to adapt and get used to workouts and therefore this is why you should chop and change the exercises that you incorporate into your workouts.

Use this as an example: remember your first dead lift? You should do because if you've never done a dead lift you have a strange routine. Anyway, remember how it felt the next couple of days when you tried to push yourself? Agonising! And then the next time you carried out this workout it felt better… and so on… maybe after 4-6 weeks of doing this same workout, your muscles weren't making the gains that you were used to. This is your muscle gains starting to plateau, in other words your body getting used to your workouts, which means you need a new one! This is where most of you are probably stuck, you have the same routines and your body is simply used to it, just like a marathon runner doesn't loose weight easily from running, because their body is used to it.

The average period of time for a person to make great gains with one workout is between 3-6 weeks, after this period of time, it would be a good idea to keep the same structure to your workouts but change the exercises a little, to shake up your muscles and kick them into gear!

Some would ask, "what happens when I run out of exercises?":

For those of you that have realised the problem that seems to be occurring in this type of training, we have a solution! For those of you that haven't…get thinking.

The only problem with this type of training is that there is a possibility that eventually you're going to run out of exercises! However if you do as advised and switch the exercises that you do every 3-6 weeks then your body will get used to them. By the time you have used up your full library of exercises you won't have done the first exercise for months and therefore you can go back and start again. Your muscles will have to get used to them again, thus having the same effect as a brand new exercise, creating a never-ending cycle of "adapt and grow" routines.

#2 "The Best Exercises"

There is large debate between athletes as to which are better:
- Compound vs. Isolation exercises
- High rep/ Low weight vs. Low rep/High weight
- Free weights vs. Static machines

Pros and cons:

Compound exercises:

Compound exercises are the utter best exercise to do if you are the type of person who wants to build even but low muscle growth upon all of your muscles. These exercises range from barbell squats, to deadlifts, to bench presses (exercises which train many muscles equally) i.e. the bench press will work your shoulders, pectorals and triceps along with some forearm stimulation.

The problem with compound exercises is that you wont get massive muscles fast, you will only get an even spread of small, lean muscle however they are great to provide you with the building blocks for further training.

Isolation exercises:

Isolation exercises are perfect for the experienced body builder or weight trainer who has already built some stable muscle foundations and would rather concentrate on the stimulation of one particular muscle group. An example of an isolation exercise would be a dumbbell curl, as you curl the dumbbell you are only stimulating the bicep (if done right) and therefore all of the muscle growth and benefits go towards that one muscle. The only problem with isolation exercises is that if you are reasonably inexperienced and haven't laid down the correct foundations first, you won't be able to lift the required weight for these to work because you'll be falling all over the place, and probably stimulating other muscle groups in the mean time!

High rep/ Low weight/resistance exercises

The great thing about high rep/low weight exercises such as a light dumbbell curl or resistance band curl is that they can cause MASSIVE muscular pumps and are generally easy to do! Great huh? However there is one problem, you'll end up getting these great pumps, and more often than not great gains, but your strength will still be pitiful! Furthermore low weight can sometimes hinder the gain that you make, if you don't mix it up with some low rep/ high weight/resistance exercises.

High weight/ Low rep exercises

High weight workouts (often for the more experienced athletes) are very difficult, for a start. To begin to do these you definitely need to have laid down solid muscle foundations before hand. However there are great pros in lifting high weights. First off it doesn't take you as long as the monotonous high rep workouts, and secondly whereas you might not get obvious pumps, you will certainly get the stimulation required for quick, lean, solid growth in your muscles.

Free weights

Free weights are great if, again, you have the muscular foundations to control yourself! If you can get your body in a stiff, controlled position when lifting, then free weights are perfect! You might even get some muscular stimulation around the other areas of your body aswell as the major pump in your chosen area. Usually with free weights you can lift quite a bit of weight, which brings me on to the problems. The only problem with lifting them is that they can be unsafe. For example if you were to drop one, it's going to hurt! Whereas a machine is a reasonably safe environment to be in.

Static Machines

The great thing about static machines is that they are safe and easy to use. Furthermore you can work your muscles from different ranges of motion, for example using a dumbbell the resistance is due to gravity, so unless you're standing on your head, the weight is always travelling down. However on a 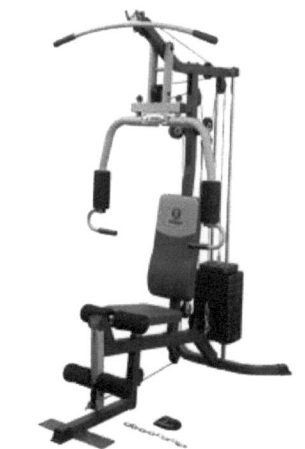 static machine, you can use the pulleys to provide upwards resistance, creating more exercises for you! As far as cons go… machines do not train your stability and therefore you can lose some stimulation in the muscles due to the restrictions but other than that machines are very good for muscle contraction. (In my workouts I use mostly free weights mainly because most of you wont have a multi-gym or smith machine at home)

Conclusion

To be honest, there is no point in "comparing" these methods because the ultimate best way to workout is to use all 6 different types of exercise… give it a try!

#3 Positions of Flexion

If you have read the previous chapter, you will be starting to classify your exercises into the different categories they fall into. However there is a deeper and much better way of classifying them.

POF is a theory developed by Steve Holman and it is a great way to group together your different exercises. It works on the basis that you train your muscles from different ranges of motion to activate the maximum amount of stimulation possible:

Mid-range power movements, Fully stretched exercises, and Peak-contraction exercises.

Mid-range power movements

A mid range movement is usually a big heavy weight compound movement such as a bench press or a dead lift. The idea behind this is that you can carry a lot more weight with mid range movements. Most of the stress and pressure in the movement is in the mid section of the exercise (hence the name) for example when you have a bench press on your chest there isn't much stress, and when you lock out your arms you get a mini-break but in the midsection, there is LOADS of stress on your muscles.

Fully stretched exercises

Fully stretched exercises are commonly isolation exercises. The theory goes that you cannot take much weight because all of the stress in at the end of the movement such as preacher curls or squats. This is yet another range of motion for your muscles!

Peak contraction exercises

Peak contraction exercises, such as concentration curls or tricep kick backs are exercises where the main contraction in the muscle is at the top of the exercise for example in a concentration curl, all of the pressure comes right at the top when you're struggling to get that dumbbell as high as it will go!

#4 How do I make my workouts more effective?

While machine exercises can be absolutely great for targeting specific muscle groups and you can do more weight with them, you can sometimes fall into the trap of doing "too many" machine exercises and losing strength. When you do a free weight exercise, your body has to stabilise you and therefore you implement crazy muscle stimulation, but a lot of the time if you do too much machine exercises you can think you're gaining strength but it will not carry over into your free weight movements because your body has become too used to not having to stabilise you.

From personal experience and opinion, the best way to go about doing a good decent workout with good stimulation and also good muscle targeting would be to base it around free weights such as barbells and dumbbells and supplement in the machine exercises when you cant train a muscle from a particular range of motion without the machine. For example a lat pull down trains your lats from the top downwards, I dare you to try and do this with a free weight? Impossible…

Attacking your muscles from 3 dimensions of training.

The "3D" theory has played a great role in giving me the incentive to mainly train with free weights. The idea is that (as partly mentioned earlier) when you train with free weights your muscles are being stimulated from ALL directions because your body has to stabilise you, pumping your blood around your body like mad! As long as you use the three positions of flexion when working out, and bare this in mind too, your muscles will be stimulated and therefore grow from all directions and you will not be left with those silly thin yet tall muscles you see some people with at the gym.

#5 Where should I train?

A lot of you reading this will be thinking "well I think I train at a fantastic gym, it has lots of modern equipment and personal trainers in abundance!" well good for you… but listen.

The average gym nowadays is a "fitness" gym where you get 90% treadmills and rowing machines and maybe the odd free weight that nobody uses. You'll also have noticed that everyone around you is VERY fit but nobody has particularly big muscles. Now don't get me wrong, these types of gyms are great for getting thin and cutting off the fat but for weight training you need a hardcore gym.

A hardcore gym will be the gym in your town or area where the bodybuilders go, the one that you'll walk in and almost cry as everyone is twice the size of you, this is the one you should be attending! For one reason they'll have SO much better equipment for making muscle gains, after all that is primarily why they're there. Furthermore you'll subconsciously be much keener to get bigger and have greater drive if you're the little one, whereas you might take a backseat in a pussy gym as you're already the biggest by far.

I'm not knocking fitness gyms because they're just there for a different reason. In all honesty I'm knocking you because you've been taking it easy at these gyms the whole time and you haven't had the support and encouragement of the ones who've been through it! In all honesty if you'd have attended hardcore gyms your whole life, you wouldn't have bought this guide, because you'd know enough already!
(Alternatively get free weights at home, and then you can't use machines)

#6 the actual workouts!

Up to now, everything you have read has been the science, explanation and reasoning for doing the Bicep Muscle Growth Guide, but now we actually get into the workouts! This is where you come in, from now on its all up to your training dedication, accuracy, and nutrition ☺

The workouts will be split into 3 phases:
- Phase one, a full body priming phase, this should last between 3-6 weeks and should completely prepare your body for hardcore workouts. Up until now you probably don't have the stability to perform the heavy lifts. And if you do, do this phase anyway because it will boost all your muscles too, aswell as increasing your bicep support. (after all this is a bicep guide)
- phase two: This is the real meat of the course. Here you will specialise on Biceps for 4-6 weeks and be able to watch your biceps grow week after week, with only 2 specialisation workouts per week.
- Phase three: This is the hardcore phase of supporting the muscle you have produced and making it stable enough to not deplete. This phase will make you a lot stronger and still increase the size and tone of your muscles.

Phase 1: Prepare your body and pack on muscle

For this phase you will workout 3 days per week, preferable Monday, Wednesday, and Friday but if this does not fit with you, any 3 **non-consecutive days** will work just as nicely.

The bread and butter of this whole phase is the Barbell squat. A great exercise that works so many muscles you wouldn't believe.

Complete 1-2 warm-up sets of about 15 reps first. This will warm your joints up and get your blood flowing for the pumps you will be receiving.

After the warm-up sets, complete a single 20 rep moderate weight set using as good form as you can manage.

The key to success here is every time you do this workout, increasing the weight on your barbell by around 5-10 pounds so that your body constantly has to adjust.

In terms of the actual exercise, take one large gulp of air as you go into the squat, this will re-enforce your torso and make the rebound at the bottom a lot easier.

Don't go to the heavy weights too fast as you'll burn out quickly and wont get the desired results. Keep the numbers simple, at 3 workouts a week, you'll be adding a lot of weight to your squat eventually.

Train to failure?

There are many circumstances where training to failure can be very helpful, such as sometimes doing isolation exercises to failure pumps your muscles and increases your gain. However in this instance it is actually counter productive as it breaks you down physically and mentally and will not allow you to make the 5-10 pound gains that you want each workout.

I have no idea if you have ever tried failing a squat… it is no fun, to cut a long story short you end up pinned on the floor in the gym looking embarrassed and you crumple under a heavy barbell. Fun? Don't think so.

This isn't what I expected?

When you picked up this Bicep guide you probably didn't think that the first exercise I explained was going to be a squat (NOTHING TO DO WITH THE BICEPS). However the squat has been proven to increase ALL of your muscle stability and is therefore a great building block to base your preparatory workouts on.

Workout continued (upper body support)

Now we are going to do some upper body, bodyweight exercises which will increase your stability, and also create higher neuromuscular activation and therefore stimulate more muscular growth.

Now you've got a choice, you can either start the next part of your workout with a set of pull-ups to failure, or you can complete a failure set of dumbbell rows. Both work similar muscles but I would go with the pull-ups to get used to your bodyweight.

More choices!:

Now rest a minute and complete a set to failure of tricep dips, or if you haven't got dip bars you can complete a failure set of push-ups (press-ups). Again both of these work similar muscles, but if you have the facilities I would definitely go for the dips, as you get unique muscle stimulation that you may not be able to see in any other exercise.

After the dips rest another minute and then get out an exercise mat and complete a failure set of sit ups (or decline sit ups if you have a bench). Note: you can use a medicine ball if you have one, this will make your failure boundaries lower and stimulate more of a pump, but wont make a massive difference.

Phase 1 made easy

(summary)

- You'll be working out 3 times a week (non-consecutive days)
- Each workout will be preceded by a 5-10 minutes intense cardio session, preferable cycling or rowing for the blood pump.
- Then rest and go into squats: 1-2 light warm up sets of about 15 reps, and then 1 working set of 20 reps with more weight
- After the squats move onto this:

1. a set of pull-ups to failure (or barbell rows)
2. rest a minute
3. a set of tricep dips to failure (or press-ups)
4. rest a minute
5. a set of normal or decline sit ups to failure with the medicine ball option
6. rest a minute
7. repeat this circuit 4 times

Stick with this for at least 4 weeks, if you feel your gains have slowed then move onto phase two.

This wasn't what you were expecting?
I know this is a bicep specialisation guide, but phase 2 will cover that, be patient. However if you are feeling impatient and you want crazy gains in your biceps, on your days of from the gym do:

75-150 total reps of resistance band bicep curls (or possible light dumbbell curls)
This will give you a massive bicep pump and start to stimulate that crazy growth.

Phase 2: The meat of the programme

Phase two is the phase where we will get to max out your bicep growth! This phase will involve 4 workouts a week, preferable in this format:

- Day1: Upper body workout
- Day2: Arm workout 1
- Day3: Rest (a lot of cardio)
- Day4: Lower body workout
- Day5: Arm workout 2
- Day6: Rest (some cardio)
- Day7: Rest (Cardio)

A man who chases two rabbits catches none:

The trip to this phase is you have to compromise. You can only specialise on one thing at a time so you have to cut back on the rest of your training, hence doing double the amount of arm training than anything else.

This will get you sleeve stretching growth in your arms and still maintain those sturdy support muscles in the rest of your body.

The good thing about this is that the rest of your body gets no smaller, it just increases less, so when you have gained the right amount of muscle on your arms you can swap to a different programme and start specialising on another muscle e.g. pectorals etc…

Day1: Upper body workout

Each exercise should include a warm-up set with lighter weights, each working set should be the same weight (the maximum you can manage to bang out the full amount of repetitions)

- Incline dumbbell or barbell bench press: 3-4 sets 10-12 reps
- One arm dumbbell rows or two arm barbell rows: 3-4 sets 10-12 reps
- Barbell shoulder press: 3-4 sets 10-12 reps
- Lateral pull-downs: 3-4 sets 10-12 reps
- Abdominal crunches with the option of medicine ball: 3-4 sets 30+ reps

Day2: Bicep workout 1

Again, each exercise should include 1-2 warm-up sets with less weight and all working sets should be the same weight (this workout will be **low weight high reps** so keep the weight sensible)

-Standing dumbbell curls

3 sets of 12-15 reps

If this can be completed easily, increase the weight for your next workout

-Close grip bench press (can be slightly decline if preferred)

3 sets of 12-15 reps

If this can be completed easily, increase the weight for your next workout

-Incline dumbbell curls

3 sets of 12-15 reps

If this can be completed easily, increase the weight for your next workout

-Skull crushers (Can be decline for difficulty)

3 sets of 12-15 reps

If this can be completed easily, increase the weight for your next workout

-Dumbbell concentration curls (standing or seated doesn't make much of a difference in stimulation)

3 sets of 12-15 reps

If this can be completed easily, increase the weight for your next workout

Start with your weaker arm, and complete the same amount of reps with your stronger arm

-Dumbbell tricep kick-backs

3 sets of 12-15 reps

If this can be completed easily, increase the weight for your next workout

Start with your weaker arm, and complete the same amount of reps with your stronger arm

Day 4: Lower body workout (one of my personal favourites for killing your muscles☺)

As usual, all exercises should be performed after 1-2 lighter warm-up exercise to get that blood going!

Leg Press or squats – 3-4 sets of 10-12 reps

Leg Extensions – 3-4 sets of 10-12 reps

Stiff Leg Deadlifts – 3-4 sets of 10-12 reps

Standing Calve Raises – 3-4 sets of 10-12 reps

Abdominal Leg Raises – 3-4 sets of 20+ reps

Day 5: Arm workout 2

The usual rule about the warm-up sets applies. The exercises in this workout should be completed with higher weight because there are fewer reps to complete.

Dumbbell Hammer curls (alternate or both)

3 sets 5-8 reps

If you can easily complete this, increase the weight next time

Reverse grip barbell flat bench press

3 sets 5-8 reps

If you can easily complete this, increase the weight next time

High resistance band bicep curls

3 sets 5-8 reps

If you can easily complete this, increase the weight next time

Dumbbell overhead tricep extensions

3 sets 5-8 reps

If you can easily complete this, increase the weight next time

Dumbbell concentration curls OR machine curls

3 sets 5-8 reps

If you can easily complete this, increase the weight next time

Reverse grip cable pull downs

3 sets 5-8 reps

If you can easily complete this, increase the weight next time

Phase 2 summary:

In my honest opinion, I think you should stick with phase two for at least 5 weeks, or until you feel that your gains aren't worth it anymore. Phase two will really help gain weight in your arms and the strength increases you will make will help you in the future whatever you are doing.

Phase 3: POWER!

If you have followed this guide properly, you should have made great gains in your arms already. However this is where the truth hits. The gains in size you have made could be astronomical but you have been doing solely light-ish weights and therefore you may not have the **strength** that you want to support the **size.**

In this section of the programme we will concentrate on solidifying the mass gains that you have made to your biceps and triceps by increasing the strength in your arms. This will greatly reduce the chances of those gains getting smaller, and will also increase the mass of your arms even more!

The truth is you've been doing full range of motion exercises so far, which are absolutely great for building mass and toning, but now we want solidness! In this section we are going to use massive weight and partial range of motion, to focus all the effort and of course stimulation on the one part of the exercise that actually toughens you up! (usually the mid range i.e. in a curl).

The way this works is you are going to do more sets of less reps with **a lot** of weight and less motion, so for example in a hammer curl you will start the curl higher up and finish lower down to only utilise the mid range area. Or in a squat you will not squat down as far. You get the idea…

Remember: The whole idea of partial range of motion is to allow your muscles to lift a much bigger weight.

Burn reps

I will summarise this quickly:
Burn reps allow a lot more stimulation in muscles; they allow you to go past your point of failure. Burn reps work by completing your set of weights and then continuing after you have reached failure, but not completing the whole rep. i.e. when completing a curl set, you lift to

failure and then do some very partial range of motion "burn reps" to pump them even harder!

The workouts

The power phase of the Bicep Muscle Growth Guide will consist of working 3 days per week, preferably Monday Wednesday and Friday if that fits your schedule.

The workouts will split up the muscle groups to try and get an even increase on all of them (biceps and triceps will be slightly intensified further).

Weekly routine:

1. **Chest, shoulders, triceps**
2. **rest**
3. **Biceps and lower back**
4. **rest**
5. **Legs and abdominals**
6. **rest**
7. **rest**

Day 1, chest shoulders and triceps:

Partial bench press lockouts:
These are similar to your average bench press BUT only do the top third of the exercise, and don't bring it down to your chest. You may use as much weight as possible for this.

Partial shoulder press lockouts:
These are also similar to normal shoulder presses but again only use the top third of the exercise, and don't bring it down to your shoulders. Again use as much weight as you can handle. Push your limits safely.

Resistance band side raises:
With a resistance band, lift your arms to the side above your shoulders, use full range of motion for this exercise, at the maximum resistance possible. When finished used burn reps.

Reverse grip tricep push-downs:
With as much weight as possible, reverse-curl the cord on the machine down all the way, only use the

bottom third of the range of motion and use the maximum weight possible. When finished use burn reps.

Weighted press ups:
Attach a weight to you and complete as many push ups as you can possibly complete. If struggling only use the bottom half of the range of the exercise.

Day 3, Biceps and Lower Back

Power lifts:
These are a variation on dead lifts. You just don't bend down very far, a few inches at the most, using the maximum weight possible.

Pull ups:

Complete as many reps as possible using burn reps, and you could also attach a weight if you are finding it easy.

Barbell rows (reverse grip)
Maximum weight, again do not bend down very far.

Power hammer curls (with burn reps)
Using burn reps use the mid range of motion and maximum weight; do not go down or up too far!

Barbell curls (with burn reps)
Again, use the mid range of motion and maximum weight, utilise the burn reps too!

Day 5, Legs and Abdominals

Squat lockouts:
Just like a normal squat but use maximum weight and do not too low or you will be crushed under a heavy barbell!

Leg press or more squats (with burn reps)

Maximum weight, only the first third of the range of motion.

Weighted standing calve raises (barbell)
Maximum weight, full range of motion, LOW reps.

Weighted sit ups
While using a heavy medicine ball or any other weights, perform sit ups with full range of motion and low reps.

Leg raises
Using half range of motion, do low repetitions of leg raises.

Phase 3 summary

Day 1:
- **Partial bench press lockouts**

5 sets 5 reps

- **Partial shoulder press lockouts**

5 sets 5 reps
- **Resistance band side raises**

5 sets 8 reps and burn reps

- **Reverse grip tricep push-downs**

5 sets 6-8 reps

- **Weighted press ups**

3 sets to failure each time

Day 3:
- **Power lifts**

5 sets 6-8 reps
- **Pull ups**

3 sets to failure
- **Barbell rows (reverse grip)**

5 sets 6-8 reps
- **Power hammer curls (with burn reps)**

5 sets to failure including burn reps
- **Barbell curls (with burn reps)**

5 sets to failure including burn reps

Day 5:
- **Squat lockouts**

5 sets 5 reps
- **Leg press or more squats (with burn reps)**

5 sets to failure including burn reps
- **Weighted standing calve raises (barbell)**

5 sets to failure
- **Weighted sit ups**

3 sets 50+ reps
- **Leg raises**

5 sets 30+ reps

Thankyou!

A big thanks to all you guys reading the guide and I hope it works out for you. Just remember to rigidly stick to the guide. For any queries, problems, or reports e-mail us at cjmuscle@hotmail.co.uk.
Thanks again,